The Weight of Cows

The Weight of Cows

MANDY COE

Shoestring  Press

Typeset and printed by Q3 Print Project Management Ltd, Loughborough, Leicestershire.
(01509 213456)

Published by Shoestring Press
19 Devonshire Avenue, Beeston, Nottingham, NG9 1BS
(0115) 925 1827
www.shoestringpress.co.uk

First published 2004
© Copyright: Mandy Coe
The moral right of the author has been asserted.
ISBN: 1 899549 97 8

Shoestring Press gratefully acknowledges financial assistance from Arts Council England

Contents

Acknowledgements

Acknowledgements and thanks are due to the editors and judges of the following magazines and competition anthologies where a number of these poems first appeared:

BBC Radio Merseyside 'First Friday', BBC Radio 4 'Poetry Please', The Blue Collar Review (USA), Dream Catcher, East Street Poets Poetry Prize, Interpreter's House, Kickstart Poets Poetry Prize, Mississippi Review (USA), The New Forest Poetry Society Competition Anthology, Orbis, Other Poetry, Petra Kenney Poetry Prize, The Rialto, Smiths Knoll.

'The Girl Who Lit the First Fire' and 'The Art of Dying' were first published in *Wicked Poems* (Bloomsbury 2002).

'Broderers' Guild Apprentice', was the winner of the East Street Poets poetry prize.

THE ART OF DYING

We were nine years old when we killed Brendan.
An enemy sniper, shot
with a sawn-off broomstick, he died
without question. And unlike other lads,

always arguing for their lives,
Brendan would lie draped
like a sandbag over the wall,
his weapon fallen from his hand.

You could even poke him
with a foot, roll him over
and thumb up the lid of one flickering eye.
We took his death for granted

– most shots going wild – knowing
we could always save
the last bullet for Brendan.
Then one day I saw him

walking past our front hedge.
You're dead! I shouted, not even
bothering to aim. But Brendan
carried on by,

followed by his dad; a towering bloke,
who scowled at me
and cocked
one meaty finger.

I didn't think twice.
And with my cheek pressed
to the sharp, damp grass, I felt
the safety of being dead.

PROTECTING HIS ROUND

He could hear an extending ladder go up
from half a mile away.
His knife and fork would clatter to the plate
and we'd listen to the back gate bang while Mam
served a glare to each of us: *Eat your food.*

He was only protecting his round
and he wasn't even our dad.
But as she scraped his dinner straight into the bin,
it felt as if we had lived here forever,
with his galvanised buckets and the blue
wooden cart wedged across the yard.

Every night he'd rinse the shammies,
pale as scrambled egg, soft as something sinful.
Mam's sister told a neighbour
that he was a saint, but went quiet,
seeing me under the table
where I hid amongst the smell of knees, worrying:

didn't saints die?
We all knew he had a way with animals,
working a brick maze of wary cats and howling dogs.
When he appeared at the edge of their sky,
he'd do this hissy-whistle
so the dogs would dance, willing
their noses to touch his hand, and cats arched
up to his wet fingers, leaving palmsful of fur.

He knew all their names:
Spike, Paddy, Bolter.
Paddy's had kittens, he'd say at supper,
then he'd tell us how many, what colour.
I don't remember Mam ever looking right at him.
Like in a panto, she was always making eyes
at some audience, as if to say: *What's he like?*

His hands were so clean, all the women
loved him for doing the corners and their vestibule glass.
Why didn't Mam see how carefully he wiped the sills?
Why didn't she let us have a kitten?
Get a van, she'd say, *do those office blocks in town.*
And he'd push himself out of his chair to go knocking up,
his pockets heavy with change.

PAPER SUBMARINE

No matter how nimble my fingers were,
no matter how thumbnail-sharp
I sliced each crease
we will not survive this.

It is cold in here. The air is pale,
heavy as milk. Our footprints leak.
Pressure pushes its grinning face
into the buckling walls.

I beg all the gods to let us rise,
break the surface in a halo of foam.
My ears pop. I wipe my nose;
there is blood.

Origami fish float past to the bottom.
A boat, a pier; sodden and sagging.
I had such faith
in these shapes. What have I done?

The possibilities of every page
were endless. Crisp white angles
of paper bridges; flotillas of ships
raced in the breeze. But even down here

I hear the screams. People, desperate
for something solid to grip:
wood, metal, land.
My god, the paper islands.

STARING FOR BEGINNERS

Drunks and dogs don't like it.
If you are caught staring, it is no good pretending
to check your watch or study the ceiling.
These are signs of a novice.

Simply shift your gaze
to a mid-distance point. Cultivating a light frown
will give the impression of deep thought.

For most sentient beings, a stare
carries voltage. The subject will sense
anything from a mild buzz to a jolt. Other symptoms
include increased heart-rate, chills
and hair becoming electro-statically charged.

Staring at part of a person's body
leaves you open to a high wattage stare-back.
Hostile stare-volleys
are to be avoided in confined spaces.

Babies under the age of three
experience stares as noise.
They can be woken from deep sleep by a stare
and will look around the room to identify its source.

Train windows are useful for bending stares
round corners. But only heavily misted glass
prevents them from being sensed.

Keep stares short.
Set a minimum distance between you and the subject.
Tip: gazing and staring are two different things.
It is vital to remember this in relationships, especially
when your partner is naked.

SETTLERS

As if this land was a fractious baby,
people came to settle it. Wet-nurses
reeking of fog and coal, they emptied carpet-bags
of cotton and gin, unrolled a sing-song tongue
that twisted the names of gods and mountains
right off the map.

The rod was not spared
and forests fell silent at the slap
of metal, hard-heeled into earth. Everywhere,
straight lines radiated – as from a child's sun
drawn in the dirt. Smoke stained the sky
and the unfamiliar sound of bells
broke the air into even chunks.
They planted seeds in rows, buried themselves
not curled, but laid out like sticks.

Their hands were rough and large, drawing
slippery babies from between pale thighs, teasing
lean cattle to mount and sire. The land sighed
under the weight of it all, its horizon
pulling back, the way furniture is cleared
to make room for a dance.

At night, music
shoved the air with the whoomph
of brushfire. Bottles smashed. Women sobbed.
A man pressed his thumbs to another man's throat.
In the morning, scars glowed white as bones
and ashes stirred in unseasonable winds.

But nothing was seasonable in this place.
Yellowed calendars from home plugged holes
where draughts snaked in. Crops fingered up
then died. Streams drew in their flow
and ran backwards, leaving dusty trails
that men travelled like roads.

This was how the rumours came,
running sour along old river beds.
This is not the right land. It's to the north.
It's over the sea.
Unsettling tales of success always
somewhere else. Neighbours tried to read
each other's eyes. In church, the pews
were sharp with elbows.

The first home was abandoned,
then another. Straight lines
blurred under weeds and animal tracks.
Barn doors swung open, banging
like the heels of a sulky child.

TAX ON STARS

The night the taxers came, the rattle
of horses' harness was heard for miles
across frost-white fields. As the men pushed
into our home, icy air clung to their coats.

With sticks and boots, they kicked aside
the kettle and spitting logs. Granddad was toppled
from his chair as with a blast of steam
the fire was doused.

The Counter's eyes were sharp, his skin
dark with years of soot and smoke.
The women flushed, the men looked away.
We had all heard the tales

of fresh mortar narrowing the chimney,
of men clinging to roofs, laying blankets
over the stacks. In silence he crossed
the still warm hearth, then tipped back his head

to gauge our square of sky. As we listened
to the scratch of his pen
marking the count, we closed our eyes,
each of us praying for cloud.

WONDROUS UGLY

When the nest-box is prised open
the parrots mimic
every frightened voice of the ark, shrieking
in a rainbow fury around the keeper's head.

But the zoo quietens when the chick
is lifted out: a creature so hideous,
onlookers can only sign and blink.
Like raw pie, its baggy skin

is pricked with rows of quills,
its head lolls under the weight
of a grey carbuncle beak. Milky eyes
boggle at a thundery Lancashire sky.

The parents turn and slowly climb away,
their brilliant colours diminished
by the wonder of their ugly child.

THREE DOGS

HIS MASTER'S VOICE

I hate music. Watch my ears,
the sight of an LP
folds them flat. The black scrape
of that silver tooth.

I would stare into the throat
of the gramophone horn
and hear in its darkness
abandoned dogs scratching to get out.

In recordings of live concerts
my ears swivel, catching a silence
broken by violin strings settling in the heat;
the clarinettist licking his lips; the whisper
of a percussionist's sleeve brushing the drum's skin.
Then the conductor's baton whip-cracks through the air
and they start... Oh,
the noise!

I am deaf now.
Music is no more than the sound
of cow-bones crunched inside my skull.
I feel it vibrate up through my teeth:
dogs hurling themselves at a door to get in.

BULLSEYE

Bill loathed skinny-boy.
I did too. Stank of fear and posh.
Boss carried him by scruff,
dead rabbit. We were happy.
Me and Boss. He kicked, drank.
Drunk, his hand would flop.
My snout under hot fingers.
He'd touch my ears, mumble, call me
Mam. At night, I was white in his black.
In gaslight, our piss polished cobbles. One day
he smelt of blood. I lost his boots
among other boots. String was slipped
round my throat. *Find Sykes.*
My breath came out like hare-screams.
Claws ripped as I dragged a chain of barking men.
They slid in my blood.
Boss boss boss boss boss.

I am still with him. His feet swing
from the sky. People throw stones.
I run. But at night I bellycreep back,
waiting for his hand.

LASSIE

The air is thick with scents,
shoes, hems trail it past bright as paint.
On the lot we wait for the sun,
every raindrop distils the scent of the cloud it comes from.
Each breath can be traced to someone's lips.
Pheromones dust the sound-man's skin like pollen.
The cameraman swings the camera too fast,
his frustration sharp as scorch. The other Lassies
are being walked nearby. One squats. She is in heat.
On the boulevard the musk of roadkill is a cone of noise.
I catch its edge, my legs tremble. The trainer smoothes
a comb through my oiled fur, each finger reeks
of the soundman. Everyone grows still.
The clapperboard cracks.
My leash is loosened.
I run.
Their tension is ripe on my tongue.
I run.
At the mine entrance – fresh wood, papier-mâché,
the Max Factor and toothpaste of the child
– I sit and bark.
Cheers burst from my audience.
They rise, clapping. Giving off a mist of relief
the way dogs shake off water when coming out of the sea.

ORDINARY ACTS IN TIMES OF UNREST

Everyone in the café suddenly leaves,
moving as if to an invisible signal,
shouldering handbags, fastening buttons.
It looks almost casual
but on the tables I notice
a full cup of coffee, a toasted teacake
with one bite taken out. Next to it,
a newspaper headline is abstracted by folds.

The tea-urn hisses on the abandoned counter.
There is a smell of scorched cheese.
I check the windows but see
only rivers of condensation. Maybe
there was a newsflash, some warning
missed. Reaching for my coat
I hear a distant siren. Closing my eyes
I listen for ticking.

With a bang
the kitchen door flies open. *Tuna melt on rye!*
A laughing couple, shaking rain from their umbrellas,
step off the street. From the restrooms, a boy
followed by a scowling mum: *How many times
must I tell you to wash your hands.*

THE GIRL WHO LIT THE FIRST FIRE

In the beginning she thought
she had been chosen to be punished.
And wondering what she might have done
to bring this on herself, she would continue
her absentminded whittling and chipping...

The pain was terrible.
Who could not try to touch
this beautiful flower, raise it to smell
the strange acrid musk. Look at her hands:
three fingers gone. Thick pink scars.

Clothes, hair, all got burnt.
Even neighbours who came too close
leapt slapping and howling into the bushes.
Shoulders slumped, she would shrug her apologies
as they crashed about in the dark.

No one talked about it directly.
No one knew the word for fire.
There was no back-slapping, thanking the gods
for a force that brought the sun out at night.
There were only small silences

that seemed to grow
whenever she was around.
But after the incident with her uncle's hut
everything changed. Shuffling their feet
in the drifts of ash the whole village gathered,

asked her kindly to leave.
So there she is. Living up the mountain.
At night, just able to see her tiny, flickering light,
the villagers huddle in a circle, pretending
not to feel something is missing.

RITES

He and his sister escaped the midday sun,
hiding in the trees and pretending
not to hear their mother's calls.
When they returned, scuffing grubby feet,
the group of women on the veranda
rose and took his sister's hand.

A grass seed was tangled in her hair.
She looked over her shoulder, pulled a face
then was swallowed
by the cool shadows of the house.
Her screams sliced through walls,
rolled through windows like an explosion of flame.

As he raced from the noise,
curtains billowed, tangled with his shadow.
Hiding in the chicken shed, empty
but for one brooding hen, he pissed
against splintered wood
and bare feet in the puddle he waited

for the women to come for him.
That evening; a feast, neighbours arriving,
the sound of laughter, the smell of roast meat.
Creeping back to the house, he ate
until he was sick, then,
food still smeared round his mouth

he crouched by his sister's bed whispering.
But although he spoke her name often,
she never turned her face
fully towards him again.

THE LAST WORD

he said at night
could not contain the initials
of his daughter's name or else
she might come to harm. Awkward,
but possible. And at first he felt
some small pride
– his will keeping her safe.

Then one morning, hearing
Rabbits, Daddy! White rabbits for luck,
he realised the first word of the day
might be as dangerous
as the last. Patiently, he vetted
morning greetings,

and began to wonder:
why only his daughter? Appalled
at the risks he could have been taking
he memorised new words,
and the list of initials grew
as the list of safe words shrank.

Eventually he took refuge in gestures,
reassuring sounds. Friends started
to seek him out: a man you could really talk to.
Wiping their eyes, they thanked him,
then left, as he struggled under the weight
of his joy: the knowledge
that he was keeping them all alive.

SHOP GIRLS

I remember the roughness of women's heels,
the smell and rasp of tights as their toes slid
into unyielding new shoes.
White tissue rustled as we unboxed each style,
presenting it for approval like a bottle of wine.

Lips pursed, the women posed
on six-inch heels, while we crouched
on nylon carpet, looking up and longing
for them to trip over and die.
Flat-footed and tired, we coveted those shoes,

so high and sharp, that wherever
you walked you left a perforated line.
At lunch-break, elbows on sticky formica,
we totted up wages and fantasised
about our big night. The shoes

would be magnificent:
spiked and glossy; virgin
soles unscratched. Like race-horses
we would clip-clop the streets. Elegant and tall,
as if filmed by someone kneeling at our feet.

CATHEDRAL TOWER

Two hundred and eighty stone steps
have corkscrewed you to this height. Staggering out
into the roar of the sky, you forget for a moment
how a straight line is walked.

In the wind your face feels stiff as a mask,
your eyes stream. Roofs and chimneys
clamour for attention,
but there are no familiar landmarks.

The river has dipped out of sight and the hills rise
in all the wrong places. You focus instead
on medieval graffiti under your fingers,
the hammered strips of lightning conductor.

A pigeon and a gargoyle pointedly ignore you
until a bell tolls the quarter-hour and the bird falls,
opening into empty air. Below
tiny people cross a square of grass,

neat as a card table. On the bench a sandwich
is being unwrapped. You bite into it,
squinting at the sky, already
doubting you were ever up there.

BRODERERS' GUILD APPRENTICE

The lilies were hell, *reticello*:
white-on-white makes you blind.
This is the largest piece we have ever created
– Flowers Of The World. Embroidered,
it will take four to fold it, five to lift it.
Our old frames toppled
under the weight of the canvas, this one
fills the room with the smell of new wood.

We work in pairs.
My partner stitches from above,
I lie on a bench underneath and pull the needle through.
The taut cloth is my sky, the silver needle quick
as a shooting star. I reach up, push it back.
A sweet rhythm, the pop and hiss of thread,
diminishing loop. Tension
must be exact.

English Bluebells this week. Up there,
in true-colour-daylight, the blues glow.
But I can't see right-side.
In the lamp's hot light I identify silks by number,
threading, tying-off, passing work from leaf to stalk.
Down here the flowers spread in a tangle
of cross-threads and knots. Fabric-dust
catches in my throat, stitches
are eclipsed by the shadow of my hands.
You have to be patient on the underside,

reach too soon and the needle bites.
Our designs have been drawn from live specimens;
botanists' sketches. The colour and shape of every petal,
every stamen must be understood. There is no room
to be vague with stitches. As apprentices
we learn how Catherine of Aragon worked
in only black and white, but for our Dutch tulip
we used thirty-eight reds.

I visit cathedrals on my Sundays off.
Passing blackened robe-chests I know
what lies within – the months of work,
miles of gold thread. My shoes squeak
as I spin on my heel and wonder
how long it took to gild the vaulted roof.

FOOL

I rule by dividing men
from their pomp.
Bare-arsed, I slide up
their ladder of order, mingling
with the life-takers, law-makers.

Touching themselves under velvet gowns,
they weigh up the size of my insult.
And in that narrow-eyed moment
there is no sound
but the faintest tremor of my silver bells.

Then they laugh,
for I am the lunatic,
the Cardinal of Numskulls.
The Lord of Misrule.

Look! The Pope is giving birth.
Panting, I squat
and drop a squirming puppy
from beneath my gown.
A circle of purple faces defines my stage.

It's got its father's eyes!
The faces swell, burst.
Through showers of spittle
I see back teeth, judge
each suck and blow of breath,
measuring...   Now it is time

to bow. Leave.
In the quiet of the passageway
I grip the iron door handle,
lay my forehead against the wood.

WINDOWS

They are familiar with our touch.
Fingers, mostly, sometimes breath.
We look, but do not see them,
our sights always seeking sky.
Ugly, most of them,

pigtailed by garish cloth, old, wooden frames
and panes sent crashing into rusty skips,
replaced with a gleam, false
as dentures. They live in families

at a family address, cousins at the sides,
teenagers out back; the outsider
relegated to the garden shed.
They speak in groans and clicks

when tugged by hands, rain and wind.
Christmas is their chance to shine,
cornered with snow, brilliant with lights.
But mostly they watch us watching

the same street, same sky. And they dream
of cathedral windows, colours arched
against the world, and everyone gazing,
not beyond, not through, but at them.

PICKPOCKET'S CONFESSION

I have stolen from the dead: my father.
I leaned over and kissed his icy brow,
the briefest touch. But at the wake,
when I pulled out my handkerchief,
love letters spilled from my sleeve.
They were meant to be buried
with him, Mother cried.

Usually I can undo what I have done.
What has been lifted
can be returned...
With a hearty slap and a tiny clink,
I slip the rings back
into my best man's pocket.

When my boss reaches the bar
I follow up behind him:
Excuse me, but you dropped this.
The traffic warden pats his coat:
My pen? Where...?
I draw it from behind his ear,
then drive away,
his watch ticking on the dashboard.

But to steal from my own dad?
Please comfort me.
Hold my hands, both, tight.
No, it's no good.
I'm sorry, I think this is yours.

OFF COURSE

My girlfriend blew me a kiss.
It never arrived.
With a gust of wind off the Mersey

it went off course. A bloke in Cammel Lairds
straightened from his welding. Smiling,
he pushed up his visor and felt

a touch like a feather on his cheek.
It was meant for me that kiss.
A good bye kiss

blown from the deck of a ferry.
I walked away without waving.
Only been gone five minutes
and she's kissing other men already.

THE TUNER

The other one was generous, the house filled
with arpeggios and scales. This one
doesn't play, doesn't want you in the room at all.
As he opens his case, the clasps snap up
– vicious. They could break a pianist's fingers.

When he pushes back the felt
I think of dentists.
His hands are remarkably pink
and he does wipe the wood when he's done,
but I go over it anyway, soothing.

If he were a blacksmith,
horses would kick out when he came by.
Maybe he is cold because he knows.
But how could he?
This time I left Rachmaninov's 3rd on the seat.
He must have seen it.

It is foolish to pay so much
when there is a cheaper, local man. But this way
it's kept to a simple transaction. No jokes
about practice. No awkward questions
about lessons.

GIVEN NAME

They surround the red washing-up bowl,
politely helping themselves to chunks of fruit:
Lemurs; Long Tailed.
We wander on
to the reptile house where we look
from the gloomy tank to the printed label.
Then from the printed label to the gloomy tank:
African Four-toed Frog.

Last day on the beach
and our pockets bulge and rattle:
Purple Topshell, Keyhole Limpet,
Common Otter Shell.
Heads bowed we shuffle
the tide-line of seaweed and tampons.
Tiny flies rise and we cheer
as we turn up a *Spotted Cowrie.*

Walking home that night
we are silenced by the grey
of a million stars: *Cassiopeia,*
the Plough, Perseus.

With relish we taste
the familiar syllables, the verifiable
spelling and sing-song code.
It's a gentle hand on a panicky brow:
Calm yourself, calm....
Everything can be broken
into small chunks of human sound.

SOULS

Dying is best done outdoors
if souls are to rise without entanglement
in lampshades and louvre blinds.
With fingers as soft
as dandelion stalks, trapped souls
pluck at sealed chimneys,
letter-box flaps, the aluminium
frames of patio doors.

For the newly dead
are easily confused, paused
by skylights and spiders' webs,
butting against them
with the force of moths.
And just as birds are warned
from panes of glass by silhouettes of hawks,
so should we steer souls to an open door
with cut-out priests,
a black card cross.

One day there will be a torch
whose light will cause
the unlined fingerprints of souls to shine.
And as if at the scene of a crime, we will see
a phosphorescent glow
dusting mirrors, pictures,
even the lids of our eyes: anything
reflecting the smallest trace of sky.

ADJUSTING TO INSECT PLAGUES

Monday. I see the yellow flash
of the school bus turning up our street
– but I am determined to save this life.
My face eclipses reflected sky as I lean over the puddle
and hook a twig under the insect's waving legs.
Does it understand?
On its back are red markings. Perhaps
it is rare. Taking hold, it pulls itself free.
I lay it on the porch-swing to dry,
run down the steps feeling like God.

Tuesday. Find two more in Grandma's room.
She was on her knees,
chasing them with a slipper
and shouting in the old language.
I scooped the insects onto newspaper,
tipping them into the darkness beyond the backdoor.

Wednesday. They are everywhere. All we hear
is the swish of yard-brooms on the sidewalk.
But as soon as a path is clear,
they spill back.
My little brother stands on the doorstep
crying: "I won't, I won't."
But he doesn't complain
when I hoist him up and carry him;
my feet crunching along the road.

Thursday. Crushed, they leave purple stains.
I walked on tiptoe at first,
then tried a sweeping shuffle.
They cling to my shoes. So now
I step down firmly, praying
that a swift, purposeful death
isn't as bad as a slow one.

Sunday. They patter like hailstones
against the church windows.
I watch my little brother playing outside,
he stamps his feet,
jumps up and down.
From here it looks like he is dancing.

SILENCING THE DOOR

Alone in their house (to water plants)
you rub their back door with margarine.
Your greased fingers trace
the hinges; the worn and thirsty
wood of the jamb.

And in this Alice-in-Wonderland
mirror of back-to-backs you glimpse
your own home, from a doorway
you've only ever seen
over the backyard wall.

And your neighbour's door is a door
that sticks. It's a door that shuts only
with kicking and grunts, the screech
of hinges and snap of bolts. Or opens
with a crash and the hot breath
of frying and canned laughter.

You have waited years
for this chance... but suddenly notice
margarine is smeared on the glass
and traces of rust from the bolts
are smudged in a red handprint,
across their clean white fridge.

RACE

The car seat sags under his weight,
he steers the taxi with one hand.
D'you mind the radio?
He has a bet on:
the four forty at Chepstow.
I watch east Manchester
slide by. We turn right, left, right,
under arches, round the roundabout.

Commentary blasts
from speakers either side of my head
as we corner, swerve, speed up.
My train leaves Piccadilly at five
and Dangerous Liaisons
is running third.
Muddy Boy
is coming up on the inside.

He overtakes,
is neck and neck with Dark Knight.
The driver strains forward and I wonder
if this is an each-way bet.
Come on! Come on! Come on!
We pass the viaduct and I am sure
we have driven up this street before.
Five minutes to go... Four.
I clutch my bags, visualising the platform,
the dash through the crowds.
Muddy Boy! Muddy Boy!

Yes Yes Yes.

Jerking to a halt at the station, the driver
pounds the steering wheel with his fists.
I push a fiver between the seats and run.

TEN PIN

As the girls puff up their cheeks
and blow out smoke, they look
like woodcuts of the wind
cornered on maps of a mediaeval world.
But their continent is tiny, car park
and bowling alley. Its sea,
a puddle where mythical beasts
are reflected in red neon curves.

Colossus – the bouncer – straddles
the entrance. Behind him is the clatter
of coins, harsh bursts of song:
plum, plum, golden bell;
bar, bar, plum.
Deeper in the gloom
comes the rolling roar of wood on wood,
the axe-strike shriek of human glee.

Figures in a nativity scene, white skittles
await each player's eye and aim.
The heartbeat pause of ball, offered up
as a votive gift, then the step, dip and swing.
Soft shoes whisper as bowlers skip back.
For everyone knows the tumbling darkness
conceals the edge of the world.

BECOMING SHORT SIGHTED

means flagging down every bus
then pretending
that the northbound bus
might go south.

Becoming short sighted
means you no longer see
the need to dust
and even the oldest
of friends look good. Hell,
even you look good.

Becoming short sighted
means that watching TV
is like listening to the radio
whilst staring at a lava lamp

and February finds you
smiling at pale drifts of litter in the park
as you call out to passers-by,
How lovely,
the first signs of spring.

LONG HAUL FLIGHT

As in the burial of pharaohs
we are laid in rows,
possessions for the afterlife
placed above our heads. Alcohol begins
its process of preservation. Digestion halts
at the waist as blood pools in our legs.
Desiccation sets in and lips crack.
Eyes click like scarab beetles
whenever we blink.
We are suspended

in a night without dawn,
our watches registering time zones
that have no meaning.
There are groans. However,
we have paid for this,
so life after death is guaranteed.
Sealed doors will hiss open
to reveal a promised land.

But for now, the earth revolves without us
and below, people stir and shiver,
as if they sense something
terrible passing overhead.

POACHING BY PAINT

We could not capture deer or fish,
pheasants, hawks or fine-bred horses.
Whether engravers or painters,
we all knew the fines
for depicting creatures of the Royal Estate.

Emblems of oak leaves could not be used,
nor diamonds, crowns, suns or castles.
The County Sheriffs held endless lists
of taxable motifs. We started instead,
to carve and weave

the common shapes
of grasses, pine cones and flying birds.
Our apprentices were set to capture
the twist of hemp rope, ripples
on water, the imprint of ploughed earth.

But avoiding the King's colours was hard.
Dye could betray you,
the dullest ochre robes glowing
blood-red under the master's chandeliers.

We longed for midwinter
when, loaded with ale and pouches of pigment,
we crept to the caves.
And there, by candlelight, sang

while painting the walls with leaping stags,
golden eagles, yellow roses
and in the middle – the King,
his arse a bright Royal red.

THE BLUE ROW BOAT

rests on a shingle beach.
You brush the warm wood seat,
hear the oars' slow creak.

You built this boat day by day,
week by week
during city park lunchbreaks

and endless shop-floor shifts.
Closing your eyes you'd sand
its curves, crouch on pebbles

licking bristles to a point
to paint a name across its stern.
And rocking gently home

on the rush-hour bus you inhale
the seaweed air, savour the sound
of your boat's name.

VANDALS

The night the weathercock
was blasted off the church steeple
the rector opened his eyes to the sound of buckshot
peppering roof tiles – hail after thunder.

Torchlight slid over tombstones
as the local constable gripped his baton.
Six foot of rusted vane, gone. Nothing found
but the cock's head. The vicar held it high
on the front page of the Herald:
"Is this the Way the Wind Blows?"

Sightseers agreed that the church looked odd.
The Norman tower suddenly squat
beneath the Victorian spire.
It's that Smith lad, the congregation muttered,
picturing the Smiths' sagging barn roof,
a headless cockerel swinging
from east to west.

An unofficial delegation was sent,
cow-sheds scoured, straw-bales split.
An eye got blacked
and slurry-tanks were dragged through with rakes.
Afterwards, muddy footprints
trailed from pub door to bar
and men backhanded foam from their lips:
Bet they've buried it.

Quartering the Smiths' back field
the metal-detectors' club swept their wands.
Tuning out the clamour of rooks they scythed
to the rhythm of the soil's buzz and squeal.
The moon rose, silvering the copse of bare oaks,
the rooks settling like clusters of leaves.
That night the earth gave up three Roman coins,
a Saxon blade and a ring, still married
by verdigris to a hacked off finger-bone.

HER DOMAIN

Picking, levering,
getting the hangnail tweezered
between teeth, pull... It bleeds.
Now the polish will sting.
This is her domain:

the dressing table, her naked face
in angled mirrors. Laying out the tools
she starts to probe the minute
landscape of her skin.
There is squeezing, wiping,

hairs are selected to be plucked,
tissues ripped from the box
then dotted with spots of blood.
Pots and jars scrape
as lids are screwed on and off.

Leaning back, she angles
her head from side to side.
It is done. As she twists the lipstick
from its black and gold case,
the child at her shoulder
makes a silent 'o' with her mouth.

SAVED FOR BEST

Through the back-hedge and over the fields
the child's silk gown drags in the mud.
The jewellery box raided, paste diamonds
are cold against her neck, earrings
cruel as seaside crabs. She is a queen,
this is drag, it is serious fun
and will never feel like this again.

Best must be saved for best.
Grandmothers did it as a duty,
hoarding unused gifts;
fossilised Lily of the Valley bath-cubes;
yellowed bottles of birthday perfume,
too expensive for more than a dab every birthday;
satin dance-shoes dead in their box.

Then there's the brooch...
The heirloom, a pale velvet ghost
marking where it lies.
Passed down through generations
of pursed lips, it carries the tale
of the one time it was worn
and the garnet lost.

The empty claw-setting stares up.
We close our eyes, picture
chandeliers, a backless frock,
click the box shut.

YOUR TIN-CAN MONSTER

The cat races so fast
it leaves its lives, one by one,
turned inside out, red and shiny
as rubber gloves. Until it is bare,
a beast of bones, clattering ahead
of the rusted devil, tied to a vertebra,
fragile as the tip of a toe.

Sleeping creatures stir,
hearing echoes of the race, then sighing
lay their head on paws.
This is not their monster.

Yours follows at a gentler pace
but still leashed tight enough to feel the buzz;
the double-bass hum that sings
the texture of every place you've been.

Some no-mark lad tied on this lot and you
have been running ever since
from the drag and clamour
that will only cease when you turn and face
that small, grubby knot.

BUTTON HILL

No warning was given
– to avoid unrest and panic buying
of Velcro, poppers and zips.
In the days following the announcement
government collectors visited every household
with an open bag, a raised eyebrow.
People drew makeshift belts tighter,
dug into pockets. Toffee tins spilled out
generations of memories. Women arrived at work
as if they had been assaulted: blouses gaping.
Safety pins were swapped for cash.

At disposal sites across the country,
workers pushed back their caps, directed
trucks on arrival. Tippers roared, pouring
hissing rivers of colour into black, earth pits.
Eventually each mound in the landscape healed,
but worms and moles still came to a halt
at this treacherous rainbow seam.
As children we played on our local hill, forgetting
how it ever got its name.

My grandmother took me there once.
She put a finger to her lips
then lifted a yellowed card from her pocket.
The row of strange shapes trembled on their stitches;
duffle coat buttons,
brown and blunt as dinosaur teeth.

ARRESTED

The ground feels like gravel,
the sky tastes like gravel. Your teeth,
raw in your cheek, bite down on gravel.
His boots, your knees,
make the noise of gravel.

Somewhere near your face
a walkie-talkie clicks and hisses.
Chunks of your hair are caught
on the silver buttons of his sleeve.
Gloved hands fold you

neatly as origami. You grow
a wing. Your arm, bent
sharply backwards lifts you
on an impossible
updraught of pain.

You must fly from this.
He thrusts you forward,
but like a boy rehearsing
the launch of a paper aeroplane
he doesn't let go.

The van is partitioned into six cells,
each the size of a portaloo.
You have a cigarette but no light.
Your neighbour unfolds a matchbox,
slides it under.

At traffic lights, you see
through the blur of reinforced glass,
shapes of ordinary people
going about a world you have fallen off.

GLASSBLOWER'S CHALLENGE

Surrounded by ranks of mermaids and seahorses
the glassblower sweats.
Flawed spirals crunch underfoot as he inhales,
then skills the blueprint in his head
down the length of his arms.

In a bucket the sea snail waits.
As the glassblower lifts the shell to his ear,
salt water trickles down his cheek. He listens
to the dead silence of an occupied sea.

When his scalpel gently bisects the shell
the naked snail twists from the light,
but there is nowhere to go
except this annealed other-place. Contrary,
midwife-fingers urge its soft body
into cool sinistral curves.

The next day, day-trippers gather at his window.
The glass galleon is gone,
so are the dolphins and the sea-monster chess set.
There is one fishbowl with a snail
clicking glass against glass. Its pulsing heart
magnified as a short-sighted eye.

ALIEN ABDUCTION #3

Once, feeling my world to be huge,
I contemplated injustices, considered
possibilities. But now I move
in smaller circles patting pockets,
double checking the front door is locked.

My areas of control
have narrowed like arteries
and I wonder
if I was captured in a column of alien light,
would I signal for them not to beam me up
until I'd scribbled notes for neighbours,
turned off the gas and bolted the back gate?

Imagine, how dizzying
to recede at warp speed without your handbag.

But seeing the infinity of space
and that fragile curve of earth,
would I submit to awe?
Or would my eyes come to rest
on alien airlocks and stop-cocks,
hands itching to reach out and check.

THE MESSAGE

From all the boys, and *This one's for you!*
It lifted the spirits. Thumbing the button, pilots
turned masked faces to each other. Smiled.
Then others wanted a say, ground-staff
and back-up crews. Straws were drawn,
so each wave of strikes carried a few choice words.
Simple messages at first, then more elaborate,
edited with sleeves and spit
– careless spelling could bring bad luck.

Keep it short, the pilots grumbled,
but soon, even off-duty crew
were redrafting thoughts on war, homesickness.
And as whole phrases
were chalked round fins and curves,
the pilots shrugged, not bothering to look.
Thumbs up were less emphatic
as three stanza poems
sliced through the clouds.

After a week of it the Brass declared
that chalk dust could foul up delivery.
More likely it was the pilot who had complained:
I'm a bomber, not a bloody postman.

DUSTING THROUGH THE AGES

In a white overall and gloves
she cleans the Victorian room.
High-collared ancestors
scowl down on this laborious task, their hands
frozen in their laps, while hers
move intimately round the gilded frames.

Twentieth century people pass,
insubstantial as spirits, but still treading through
real dirt and dust. A stuffed spaniel sleeps
by the red light-bulb fire, knowing
that varnished cakes don't drop crumbs.

The fenworker's home is easier to keep:
stone flags, shepherd's crook, coffin-shaped crib.
A brace of bloodied rabbits
hang from the beam, guarded by the sheepdog,
whose begging eyes need a daily wipe
so they can catch the light.

The keening-wind plays in a constant loop
as a family in neon anoraks rustles past.
The child points at the woman:
Look mummy, a ghost.
Glenn Miller's *Little Brown Jug*
echoes up the stairs. There's still the 1940s to do.

WHEN THE EARTH LET GO

On the first day it was like being in love,
each step a little lighter. Wine poured,
thick as honey. Sagging flesh seemed to lift.
Apples lay in the grass unbruised
and when the broken-hearted jumped
it wasn't to their death.
Grocers narrowed their eyes at the scales,
tapping on a few more grains.
Airline pilots frowned, easing off the throttle.
Rain didn't fall
but hung as mist. The tides went out,
then out some more. Grandparents rose
from armchairs to dance.

It didn't last.
We burn with shame at that first joy.
Now, roped to trees and rooftops we float,
hands grasping like starfish at whatever passes.
But we can only hold on to so much.
Rivers of mud and fish rise
through a broken dome of sky. Animals moan
as they scrabble in the littered air.
We pray for a return of the earth's pull,
but at night the stars circle
under our feet, while round our heads
tears and snot curl in ribbons, silver
speech bubbles emptied of words.

READING BACKWARDS

This is the letter
that brings the news.
She licks her thumb, flicks

slowly back to the page
where she is told.
Curious

how she hadn't known
at the top of the page
– but at the bottom

everything
is changed. She counts;
39 lines, 23 commas, 10 full stops.

Resting
on her palm, the pages slowly unfold,
a shell opening.

She makes herself read the letter
backwards. Beautiful, almost
a poem.

But reaching the top,
above *We are so sorry…*
Above the address

there is just white space.
Nothing
has been undone.

FALL

From a cobweb on the ceiling
one insect wing spins, flashing
a silver morse code, an asymmetrical
blueprint of veins.

I hold up my hand to block
a slice of sun cutting through
diamond windows. In the deep glow
of my flesh I see red shadows of bones.

Everything is mapped, even this house.
In cobalt blue, diagrams of this hall,
the zigzag of these very stairs, rest
in some council plan-chest drawer.

My face is gritty against the lino,
I arrived here like a Day Of The Dead
skeleton snipped from its strings.
The film of my journey rewinds

with a long-shot of the top step,
a close-up of my feet. One of those shoes
now rests at my side, sole-up
as if disclaiming something.

The house is empty and the floor
cold. As if making angels in snow,
I test my limbs, trying
to guess what shape I am now.

LISTENING TO BEES

See; against the light – *same again please* –
how these fingerprints dull the gold of the Scotch.
Should go home now, must go home.

I'm checking the worker-traps at dawn:
the rape field, pine-woods,
that last scrub of heath along the by-pass.

Bees. Wife says I'm obsessed with them.
What do you expect? I tell the back of her head.
It's my job, I tell the closed door.

In Ireland, when my great-grandfather died
I was sent to tell the bees. By the hive
the humming air goose-bumped my bare legs.

But what to say? Now the bees tell me.
They bring clues; microscopic truths. I copy them
onto charts: pollen samples, colony reductions...

No one reads them. Hey, does anyone here
want to know what the bees are saying? It's all in my file:
Min of Ag label, tatty edges, third shelf up.

THE WEIGHT OF COWS

Cows are impossibly heavy,
they are the dark matter
that astrophysicists talk of.
All the weight of the universe
can be accounted for, if
you include cows.

It is this weight that splays
hooves deep into the mud,
draws milk down to bursting
udders, makes cow pats slap
the earth with uncanny force.

Even milked-out
they move heavily.
Arching knuckled backs
under the sting of the auctioneer's stick,
they buckle and stagger
as if their very bones
were recast from bedsteads,
rusted park railings.

To see a cow hoisted
into the air by one hind leg
is to witness
the death of a planet.

THINGS TAKE UP MORE SPACE WHEN THEY ARE MISSING

It starts as a summer barbecue.
Dad is mesmerised by the flames.
Even when the rusty grill topples
he just kicks the coals into a pile,
then drops the oven glove on top.
Bonfire, he grunts.

He throws on some broken fencing
and us kids start breaking up the deckchairs.
Inching sideways down the back step
Grandma tells empty air
how she always baked potatoes
on Guy Fawkes' night.

Sam rubs tears and ash across his face.
Doing a stiff little dance, he suddenly kicks
the shoes mam bought him into the blaze.
We open our mouths, but no one speaks.

Dad drags over mam's wooden barrow
and, in a whoosh of sparks, tips the whole thing
into the fire. The girls are crying
as they come out carrying the china dog,
a tablecloth, a handful of yellow Hoover bags.
Grandma claps: *Get the Guy. Get the Guy.*
Dad fetches the Hoover.

The next morning, empty spaces startle us.
We shift furniture to cover dents in the carpet,
stick posters over bright squares of wallpaper.
Upstairs, we put dad's pillow
in the middle of the bed and draw his clothes
screeching along the rail to fill out the wardrobe.

IN THE TONGUES OF GUNS

Fluent in firearms these boys spoke
a language that overcame all divisions of class.
With perfect diction they shared
epic, wordless plays. Soundscapes composed
of mortar fire, the rattle of machine guns,
heavy artillery.

On the back field,
an audience of girls waited
to apply folded dock leaves to the wounded.
Then Sally Fisher broke all the rules.
Shouting *I'll kill them all,* she leapt up,
hurled a hand-grenade over their heads.

I'm Boadicea not a spy,
she sing-songed later,
tugging at the hem of her school skirt.
But the boys decided
she had shouted bang instead of boom,
so the grenade had misfired.

Wearing a necklace of yellow leaves,
Sally Fielding was hanged from the willow tree,
then rehanged until she agreed
to make the sound of her own neck breaking.

THE CHOCOLATE POLISHER

Last in the line
of dollopers and makers, I create
the unblemished sheen
revealed as each lid lifts
with a rustling yawn.

I manufacture the illusion,
wipe away clues of anonymous haste:
the screaming clank and heat;
the sickly-sweet air that clings
to our clothes. All fingerprints

are erased with my quick
white gloves, my soft cloth.
Lift, wipe. Lift, wipe. Every chocolate
laid to rest in the dark, innocent
as a closed eye.

I picture a woman,
the open box resting in her lap.
Her fingers hover as she decides.
It is proof of my skill: that trust,
her belief in this perfect hush.

BEFORE NUMBERS

you would use your hands,
spreading fingers to weigh a guess,
laying palm to palm to seal a bargain.

Envy was no more than visions
of a silver cup, a woman's lips,
white cattle in an emerald field.

Before numbers, generals and thieves
measured dominion by rumour. Borders
growing more distant on dull expeditions.

Before numbers each death had a name
and made no sense beyond the overwhelming
loss of one. Had you whispered the word *millions,*

you might have been mistaken
for someone at prayer, or a messenger
practising the title of a foreign monarch.

Before numbers no one knew who won the war.
Even with a knife to help you measure it,
no length of wood could hold so many cuts.

OTHER BOOKS FROM SHOESTRING PRESS

POEMS Manolis Anagnostakis. Translated into English by Philip Ramp. A wide-ranging selection from a poet who is generally regarded as one of Greece's most important living poets and who in 1985 won the Greek State Prize for Poetry.
ISBN 1 899549 19 6   £8.95

HALF WAY TO MADRID: POEMS, Nadine Brummer *Poetry Book Society Recommendation*. ISBN 1 899549 70 6 £7.50

WAITING FOR THE INVASION: POEMS, Derrick Buttress
ISBN 1 899549 69 2   £6.95

TESTIMONIES: NEW AND SELECTED POEMS Philip Callow. With Introduction by Stanley Middleton. A generous selection which brings together work from all periods of the career of this acclaimed novelist, poet and biographer. ISBN 1 899549 44 7
£8.95

PASSAGE FROM HOME: A MEMOIR Philip Callow. Angela Carter described Callow's writing as possessing "a clean lift as if the words had not been used before, never without its own nervous energy." ISBN 1 899549 65 X   £6.95

Shoestring Press also publish Philip Callow's novel, BLACK RAINBOW.
ISBN 1 899549 33 1   £6.99

TARO FAIR, Ian Caws
ISBN 1 899549 80 3   £7.50

INSIDE OUTSIDE: NEW AND SELECTED POEMS Barry Cole. "A fine poet ... the real thing." *Stand*. ISBN 1 899549 11 0   £6.95

SELECTED POEMS Tassos Denegris. Translated into English by Philip Ramp. A generous selection of the work of a Greek poet with an international reputation.
ISBN 1 899549 45 9   £6.95

COLLECTED POEMS Ian Fletcher. With Introduction by Peter Porter. Fletcher's work is that of "a virtuoso", as Porter remarks, a poet in love with "the voluptuousness of language" who is also a master technician. ISBN 1 899549 22 6   £8.95

KAVITA, TF Griffin. ISBN 1 899549 85 4   £6.50

LONG SHADOWS: POEMS 1957–2000 JC Hall. ISBN 1 899549 26 9   £8.95

SEVERN BRIDGE: NEW & SELECTED POEMS, Barbara Hardy.
ISBN 1 899549 54 4   £7.50 Second Printing

CRAEFT: POEMS FROM THE ANGLO-SAXON Translated and with Introduction and notes by Graham Holderness. *Poetry Book Society Recommendation*.
ISBN 1 899549 67 6   £7.50

ODES Andreas Kalvos. Translated into English by George Dandoulakis. The first English version of the work of a poet who is in some respects the equal of his contemporary, Greece's national poet, Solomos. ISBN 1 899549 21 8   £9.95

FIRST DOG Nikos Kavvadias. Translated into English by Simon Darragh
ISBN 1 899549 73 0   £7.95

A COLD SPELL Angela Leighton. "Outstanding among the excellent", Anne Stevenson,
Other Poetry. ISBN 1 899549 40 4   £6.95

THE FIRST DEATH Dimitris Lyacos. Translated into English by Shorsha Sullivan. With
six masks by Friedrich Unegg. ISBN 1 899549 42 0 £6.95

WISING UP, DRESSING DOWN: POEMS, Edward Mackinnon.
ISBN 1 899549 66 8   £6.95

TOUCHING DOWN IN UTOPIA: POEMS, Hubert Moore
ISBN 1 899549 68 4   £6.95 Second Printing

MORRIS PAPERS: Poems Arnold Rattenbury. Includes 5 colour illustrations of Morris's
wallpaper designs. "The intellectual quality is apparent in his quirky wit and the skilful
craftsmanship with which, for example, he uses rhyme, always its master, never its servant."
Poetry Nation Review. ISBN 1 899549 03 X   £4.95

THE ISLANDERS: POEMS, Andrew Sant ISBN 1 899549 72 2   £7.50

BEYOND THE BITTER WIND: Poems 1982–2000, Christopher Southgate.
ISBN 1 899549 47 1   £8.00

GIFTS OF EGYPT: POEMS, Michael Standen ISBN 1 899549 71 4   £7.95

MEDAL FOR MALAYA: a novel David Tipton.
ISBN 1899549 75 7   £7.95

PARADISE OF EXILES: a novel David Tipton.
ISBN 1899549 34 X   £6.99

STONELAND HARVEST: NEW AND SELECTED POEMS Dimitris Tsaloumas. This
generous selection brings together poems from all periods of Tsaloumas's life and makes
available for the first time to a UK readership the work of this major Greek-Australian
poet.
ISBN 1 8995549 35 8   £8.00

COLLECTED POEMS, Spyros L. Vrettos
ISBN 1 899549 46 3   £8.00

For full catalogue write to:
Shoestring Press
19 Devonshire Avenue
Beeston, Nottingham, NG9 1BS UK
or visit us on www.shoestringpress.co.uk